JUN 16

L6
3.1
0.5 points

LIGHTNING
BOLT
BOOKS™

Can You Tell a Cricket from a Grasshopper?

Buffy Silverman

Lerner Publications Company
Minneapolis

Lerner Publications Company
A division of Lerner Publishing Group, Inc.
241 First Avenue North
Minneapolis, MN 55401 U.S.A.

Website address: www.lernerbooks.com

Library of Congress Cataloging-in-Publication Data

Silverman, Buffy.
     Can you tell a cricket from a grasshopper? / by Buffy Silverman.
        p.   cm. — (Lightning bolt books.™— Animal look-alikes)
     Includes index.
     ISBN 978-0-7613-6736-9 (lib. bdg. : alk. paper)
        1. Crickets— Juvenile literature. 2. Grasshoppers— Juvenile literature. I. Title.
     QL508.G8S525 2012
     595.7'26— dc23   2011022546

Manufactured in the United States of America
2 — PP — 6/1/12

Table of Contents

Antennas: Long or Short?

Crickets and grasshoppers look a lot alike. Their back legs are long and strong. Long legs let them jump far.

Do you see this cricket's long back legs?

Crickets and grasshoppers are insects. Insects walk on six legs. Their bodies have three main parts.

Grasshoppers have six legs.

5

But you can tell these insects apart. Look at this grasshopper. Short antennas stick out from its head. Insects smell and feel with their antennas.

This grasshopper's short antennas wave in the air.

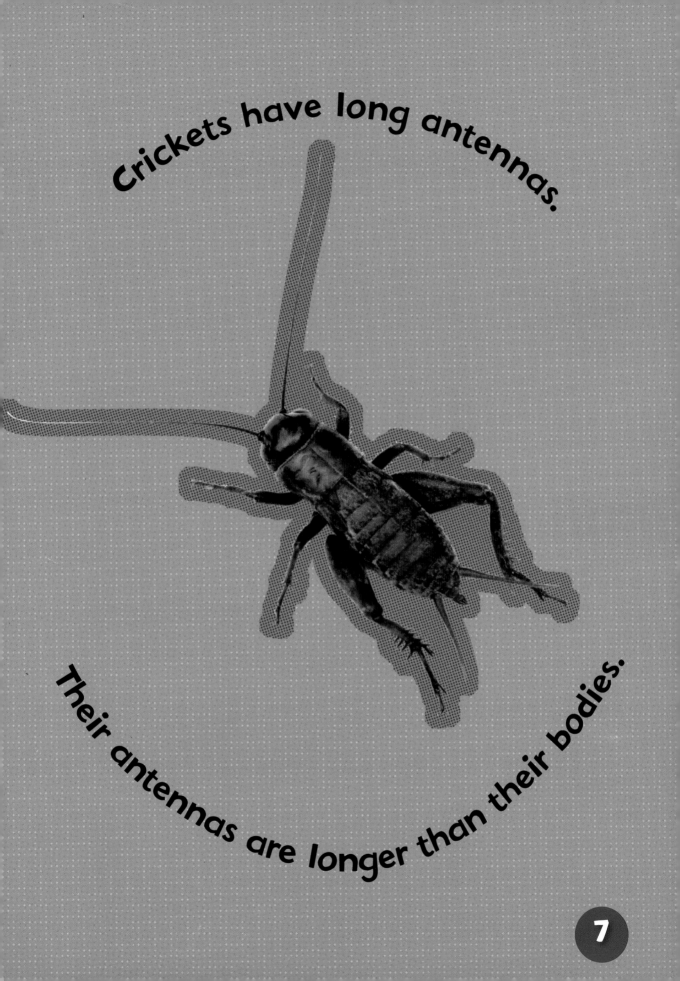

Crickets have long antennas.

Their antennas are longer than their bodies.

7

Singing: Night or Day?

Open a window on a summer night. Do you hear chirping? Crickets are singing. Most crickets sing after sunset.

Grasshoppers sing during the day. You can hear them in a field on a sunny day. They make a buzzing or scraping sound.

Listen while crickets and grasshoppers sing. You can pick out different songs. Every kind of cricket and grasshopper sings a different song.

This grasshopper sings a different song than other kinds of grasshoppers.

Usually only males sing. Their songs tell females where to find them. A male mole cricket sings from his tunnel. His tunnel is shaped like a horn. It makes the sound louder.

A male meadow grasshopper sits on a blade of grass. He sings a loud song. The female answers with a soft chirp.

This female meadow grasshopper listens to a male sing.

Songs also tell other males to stay away. A male cricket hops away when he hears another male calling.

This cricket doesn't like other males to get too close.

Singing: Legs or Wings?

How do grasshoppers sing? Most rub their hind leg against their front wing. They have a row of teeth on the leg. The teeth scrape against a ridge on the wing.

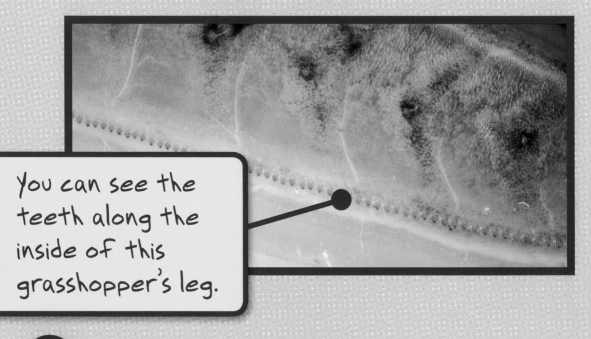

You can see the teeth along the inside of this grasshopper's leg.

Crickets sing with their front wings. A row of teeth sits along the wings' bottom edge. The top of the wing has a ridge. A cricket chirps by rubbing the teeth over the ridge.

This cricket chirps by rubbing its wings together.

Some grasshoppers sing
while flying. Band-winged
grasshoppers snap their back
wings together. They make a
crackling sound.

Grasshoppers listen to other grasshoppers' songs. A grasshopper's ears are on its abdomen. The abdomen is the last part of its body.

This is the grasshopper's ear.

A cricket's ears are on its front legs. A female cricket listens for males of her own kind.

This is the cricket's ear.

Growing Up

Grasshoppers and crickets begin life as eggs. This grasshopper lays her eggs in the fall. She has a short tube for laying eggs.

A grasshopper lays a group of ten or more eggs.

A cricket's egg-laying tube is longer. This cricket pushes her tube into the soil. She lays one egg at a time.

This cricket lays eggs using the long tube on her body.

Grasshopper and cricket eggs
hatch in spring or summer.
The insects that hatch are
called nymphs. Nymphs look
a lot like their parents.

Grasshopper nymphs chew grass and other plants. They grow as they eat. But their hard skin can't stretch.

They shed it. Then they can grow bigger.

This grasshopper nymph eats a leaf.

Crickets chew plants too. But they also eat animals they find. This cricket nymph chews on other insects.

Nymphs can't fly or sing. Their wings aren't fully grown. This grasshopper nymph has small wing pads. The wing pads grow each time it sheds its skin.

Wing pads are body parts that grow into wings.

This grasshopper nymph is shedding its skin.

Shedding skin is called molting. A grasshopper molts four or five times. Then it becomes an adult. Many grasshoppers take one to two months to grow.

Crickets molt eight to twelve times. They grow for two or three months before becoming adults. A cricket's wings unfold after its final molt. Then it can rub its wings and chirp.

This cricket is finishing its final molt.

Crickets and grasshoppers leap in fields and meadows.

Can you tell these look-alikes apart?

Who Am I?

Look at the pictures below. Which ones are crickets? Which ones are grasshoppers?

My antennas are short.

My antennas are long.

I sing after sunset.

I sing during the day.

I rub my leg against my wing to sing.

I rub my wings together to sing.

column 2: cricket, grasshopper, cricket
column 1: grasshopper, cricket, grasshopper
Answers:

Fun Facts

- Many grasshopper songs are too high-pitched for humans to hear. But other grasshoppers can hear them.

- The snowy tree cricket is called the thermometer cricket. People tell the temperature by counting its chirps. They count the number of chirps in 15 seconds. Then they add 37. This gives the temperature in degrees Fahrenheit.

- Crickets can be right-winged or left-winged! Some rub their right wing over their left wing. Others rub their left wing over the right one.

- When grasshopper nymphs are crowded, they bump into one another. That can cause them to act differently. They may even turn a different color. Then the grasshoppers are called locusts. They travel together in huge groups.

Glossary

abdomen: the last part of an insect's body

antenna: a feeler on an insect's head. An insect smells and feels with its two antennas.

hatch: to break out of an egg

insect: an animal that has six legs and three main body parts as an adult

molt: to shed old skin

nymph: a young insect that changes gradually into an adult. A nymph looks like its parents, but it does not have fully grown wings.

wing pad: part of the body on a nymph that will become the wing

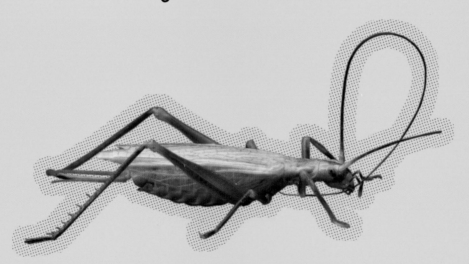

Further Reading

Allen, Judy, and Tudor Humphries. *Are You a Grasshopper?* New York: Kingfisher, 2002.

Cricket Printout
http://www.enchantedlearning
.com/subjects/insects/orthoptera/
Cricket.shtml

Glaser, Linda. *Singing Crickets.* Minneapolis: Millbrook Press, 2009.

Grasshoppers and Relatives
http://www.biokids.umich.edu/
critters/Orthoptera

Hansen, Amy S. *Bugs and Bugsicles: Insects in the Winter.* Honesdale, PA: Boyds Mills Press, 2010.

Insect Sounds
http://www.naturesongs.com/
insects.html

Index

Photo Acknowledgments

The images in this book are used with the permission of: © INSADCO Photography/ Alamy, p. 1 (top); © Don Farrall/Photodisc/Getty Images, p. 1 (bottom); © Minden Pictures/SuperStock, pp. 2, 26; © David M. Dennis/Animals Animals, p. 4; © NHPA/ SuperStock, pp. 5, 10, 27 (bottom), 28 (bottom left); © Luis Castaneda Inc./The Image Bank/Getty Images, pp. 6, 28 (top left); © Melinda Fawver/Dreamstime.com, pp. 7, 28 (top right); © Premaphotos/naturepl.com, pp. 8, 28 (center left); © age fotostock/ SuperStock, pp. 9, 28 (center right); © A & J Visage/Alamy, p. 11; © Kim Taylor/ naturepl.com, pp. 12, 27 (top); © imagebroker.net/SuperStock, p. 13; © Gilles San Martin, p. 14; © Peter Waters/Dreamstime.com, pp. 15, 28 (bottom right); © Satoshi Kuribayashi/Nature Production/Minden Pictures, p. 16; © Anthony Bannister/NHPA/ Photoshot, p. 17; © Jerome Wexler/Visuals Unlimited, Inc., p. 18; © Doug Wechsler/ Animals Animals, p. 19; © A.N.T. Photo Library/NHPA/Photoshot, p. 20; © Raymond Mendez/Animals Animals, p. 21; © Carroll W. Perkins/Animals Animals, p. 22; © PhotoAlto/Alamy, p. 23; © Michael Turco/Visuals Unlimited, Inc., p. 24; © James H. Robinson/Photo Researchers, Inc., p. 25; © Joel Sartore/National Geographic/Getty Images, p. 30; © Andrey Nedelchenko/Dreamstime.com, p. 31.

Front cover: © Joel Sartore/National Geographic/Getty Images (top); © Teresa Kenney/Dreamstime.com (bottom).

Main body text set in Johann Light 30/36.